Sex Positions in Pictures:

25 Sensual Kama Sutra Positions Illustrated for Hotter, More Satisfying and More Fun Sex

By Emily Ward

Sex Positions in Pictures by Emily Ward. Published by Walnut Publishing Company, Hanover Park, IL 60133

Walnutpub.com ← Sign up for FREE books

Table of Contents

Introduction & Tips

First of all, thank you for downloading our sex positions guide! We hope you will have fun exploring all the new positions included in this book.

So: Are you ready to have the sex life you've always wanted? It's time to freshen things up and discover what you've been missing in the bedroom. If you've been doing the same positions over and over, you can explore 25 new, fresh sex positions in the following pages.

PLUS! You also get 5 bonus oral sex positions.

Turn up the adventure, steaminess and, most importantly, fun in your sex life — you and your partner will be glad you did.

Before we dive into the 20 positions, here are a few tips:

Try something new just for the sake of it
Sometimes, trying something new, even if it isn't the best position in the world, will be extra fun just because it's new. Mixing things up will feel adventurous and sexy, even if you try a position that you won't use regularly.

Communicate
The best way to ensure success with these positions is to have open communication with your partner, so both of you can speak up when something isn't working well for one of you. A position that isn't feeling exceptionally sensual could maybe become a new favorite with a slight adjustment. Be willing to open up!

Go slow if you need to
Some readers will want to try all of these tonight — some may want to sprinkle them in. Go at your own pace!

Welcome, male readers!
While the descriptions in this book use "you" to refer to the female partner, each position applies to heterosexual couple and is illustrated for ease of understanding, so get reading, and be the one to introduce new positions, guys! This book is for you, too.

Use precaution!
If a position seems too difficult, don't risk your safety! Always keep in check that you performing positions within your physical limits.

Alright, let's get to the FUN stuff. Enjoy! ;)

BONUS: Subscribe to the Free Book Club at **www.walnutpub.com** *for more books from author Emily Ward, and free new releases from Walnut Publishing.*

25 Sex Positions with Pictures

1. The Star

This position is a variation on missionary, but don't let that fool you into thinking it's boring! In this one, lie on your back. Have one leg outstretched straight in front of you, with the other bent up like an "L". Have your partner sit facing you. One of his legs goes under your bent "L" leg, and the other wraps around your outstretched one. The position will look similar to a star (makes sense, right?) when done right. Do this one if you want some great G-spot stimulation, as you'll feel more than you ever could in regular missionary! Your clitoris will also be more open to him — or you — for manual stimulation. This position will feel familiar, but new and exciting at the same time.

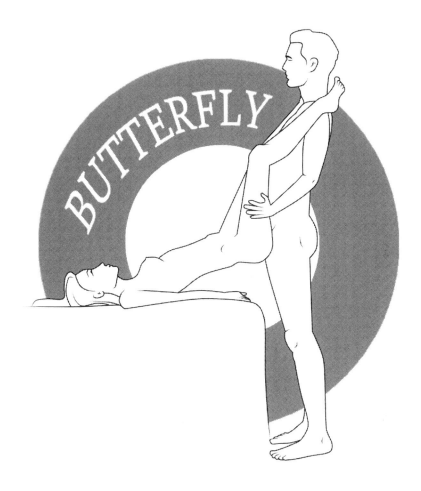

2. Butterfly

Move your hips to the edge of the bed, as your partner stands facing you. Put your ankles on his shoulders, but keep your thighs together. Keeping your legs together may be a bit difficult, but worth it! This gives him extra stimulation and will feel intense for both of you. You don't have to do much in this position, and probably won't be able to. For an added bonus, add a pillow or two underneath your butt — this will give him added control and he moves in and out. So let him take control in this one. Switch this one up by having him kneel on the bed instead, or moving both of your feet to one of his shoulders.

4

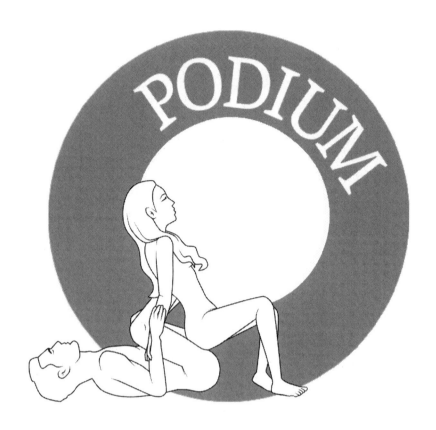

3. Podium

Podium is almost like doggy style, but rotated — your guy will be on his back. To try out this position, have him lie on his back and pull his knees up to his chest. You will sit on him almost like a chair, supporting your body weight with your legs out in front of you, bent, and your arms down at your sides on his legs or holding his hands or arms. You'll be in control here, so add this to the list of ultimate girl power positions. Thrust your pelvis upward and command the action.

4. Roman Column

This one can be a bit of a balancing act — so only attempt if you're sure you've got the balance and the strength to pull it off! For this one, you'll use the corner of the bed. He will sit on the corner of the bed facing outward, so his legs are spread and draped over either side of the bed. You'll squat on the very corner of the bed, facing away from him, and he enters you from behind. With his legs touching the floor, he'll get more thrust in this position than both of you sitting in a chair or crouching on the bed. You, with your feet on the bed, can also help thrust. Just don't get too wild, and hold on. The last thing you want is someone tumbling off the edge here.

6

5. Amazon

You will feel locked in together like puzzle pieces in this high-intensity position. In this position, have the guy lie on his back and pull his knees toward his chest. You then fit into him like a puzzle piece. Rest your thighs on his, with his heels on either side of your waist. You can hold onto his knees for balance, and tuck your legs behind your body for added stability as well. He'll need to move his penis down a bit to enter you, and rotate your hips to help here. This position sounds a bit complicated, but trust us, once you get it, it is a whole new experience. Some say this is the closest you'll feel to being the man during sex outside of adding toys into the mix.

6. Pony

This one may work best on the floor for some stabilization. Your man kneels on one leg while he has his other foot flat on the floor in front of him, with his knee bent. Kneel on one of your knees as well, the opposite of his, and drape the other over his leg that is bent forward. Penetration may be a bit tricky here, but this one is a great opportunity to explore literally getting down and dirty. (Pro tip: Do this one on the carpet to avoid pain and aches later!)

7. Crouching Tiger

Switch things up with this advanced position for an extra steamy and gratifying sex session. Though it looks difficult, this one is easier than you might think. Lie down, and have your partner slowly pick up your ankles, pulling them back over and above your face, so that your back raises and you are effectively resting on your shoulders. With your vagina facing toward the ceiling, he stands over you, bending his knees a bit to enter you from above. He can continue holding your ankles to keep everything stable. He'll have to control all the movement here, as you'll be a bit immobilized. But call yourself an expert on wild sex positions after trying this death-defying, upside-down and adventurous one!

8. Lock and Key

You'll fit together like a perfect lock and key combination in this experiment. In this position, your man lies on his side, and enters you from a right angle. You are therefore perpendicular to his body, and he can swing his arm under your thighs to help move you back and forth for some controlling play. It may be difficult for you to control your movement as much in this one, but it is a restful position that can help both of you take a little break while still feeling connected if you've been in a sex session for quite a while.

9. Ferris Wheel

For this one to work, your partner will lie down on his back with one knee bent and the other leg straight. Mount him sideways, so that your clit is facing his bent leg. This allows for you to rock and ride his leg with your clit, giving you some intense stimulation and pleasure, while he's inside you and can feel your intensity as well. Place your other knee in-between his legs, so you're facing sideways from his perspective, or straddle him reverse cowgirl style, so he sees the back of your head, and play with his balls, something to heighten this tantalizing and teasing position.

10. Panther

This steamy position achieves maximum closeness of your bodies,
while at the same time being at totally separate ends of the
encounter. He lies down, facing upward. You straddle him in the
reverse, and then lean forward, swinging your legs behind you and
up by his ears. His feet will be by your ears as well. So you are
effectively lying on each other, but your bodies in opposite
directions. You will be able to move together, but you'll ultimately
have more power in this one over him. It might be tricky to keep him
inside, so some clenching here from you will keep him there.

11. Torch

Get ready to light a fire with this one, which is similar in style to the Panther position (position no. 10). He sits up, and his legs are out in front of his body. You straddle him, facing away, as though you were doing reverse cowgirl. But here's where things start to heat up. Lean forward, and straighten your legs behind you. You can both rock backward and forward for some explosive orgasms, and he can pull on your hair, smack your rump, or just rub all up on your back for some satisfying closeness.

12. Rhombus

He lies on his side, and you lay opposite him, with your head near his feet and your feet near his head, such as in the 69 position. Wrap your legs around him and hug his knees to your chest. You are slightly curled up, and your butt will be right below his face, which can be extra exciting for him. But your head will be near his feet, so make sure that doesn't bother you!

13. Downward-Facing Dog

This simple twist on the classic doggy style helps to guide the tip of his penis to your G-spot. To do this pose, have him enter you from behind like regular doggy style, but then lean down your shoulders and stretch your arms in front of you so that your back is arched (this may require some flexibility, so just go as low as you can. It doesn't take a severe angle to get all the benefits of this new position. Get an assist from a pillow underneath your chest if the angle is too much). This will enable him to go deep. Another added bonus is that not being able to see each other's faces can increase the sensuality here. But you can also do this one in front of a mirror to keep a visual on each other. You also both have extra use of your hands for fondling and stimulation — you can touch yourselves, or each other.

14. Waterfall

This position can be interchanged for either partner — but careful! It might involve a rush to the head, but in a good way? Either the woman or man lays off the edge of the bed so that the crown of his or her head is pointing towards the floor. Yes, upside-down, just be careful not to fall! This position may be difficult for either of you to sustain if you get dizzy easily, but the head rush also means a new perspective on the pleasures and sensations of sex, and hey, maybe it will become one of your favorites! Some experience more ecstasy in this position with blood rushing to his or her head, and there's only one way to find out if you like it!

15. Envelope

In this position, both partners lie on their sides. The woman pulls
her legs up to her chest. If you're flexible, you may be able to do this
with straight legs. For most people, you'll need to bend your knees!
Your partner enters you, and from this position is able to caress your
clitoris as well. Or, he can wrap his arms fully around you, and the
sensation of being totally enveloped while he thrusts in and out will
produce a rapid fire of pleasure hormones for both of you.

16. The Frog

We know...this doesn't sound sexy. But ladies, this one is all about your pleasure. You are on top, with your legs on either side of your guy. Don't straddle him with your calves and feet folded behind you — instead, squat so that your legs are in front of you. This will take some extra leg muscle, but the clenching of all your lower body muscles will enhance the sensations for you and him. Focus your attention on using your inner-vaginal muscles to squeeze him, and you can also control the speed and intensity of your thrusting, and have more control over climax. Another bonus — this position is great for deep penetration. To stay balanced, you can put your hands on your man's chest, legs, stomach or rib cage to get support. Try alternating with just the tip to deep penetration. You'll feel this one all along the inside walls of your vagina.

17. Lotus Blossom

Like the reverse cowgirl position, your man lays down on the bed and you are on top, facing away from him. You can kneel, but lean forward and balance yourself by putting your hands on his knees. Though similar to the famous reverse cowgirl position, the added act of leaning forward a little bit will increase your pleasure and his in this new angle. Try moving back and forth, having his penis enter and leave you, instead of up and down. The slight variation will allow for a familiar rhythm but a new angle and new sensations.

18. Hip Raise

He kneels on the bed, and you wrap your legs around him. Arch your back and lay down on the bed. You'll both work to support your body as he pulls your butt up off the sheets. This position allows for him to hold you underneath your lower back and move you in and out as he pleases. This is a flattering angle, as your body is spread eagle with your breasts in full view for him to take in. It also allows for deep penetration, which can feel amazing for him, but if it's too deep, you can also pull back a bit as he thrusts. You should both have control in this satisfying maneuver.

19. The Curl

This one is cuddly, so get ready for a lot of intimate touching.
Almost like spooning, in The Curl, you will pull your knees to your
chest, and his knees will be outside yours. His body will shape to
yours, with contact everywhere. He enters you from behind, and this
makes for a lot of pleasurable kissing on your neck and head and
rubbing and holding of your body. This is an excellent, relaxing
position during which he can be inside you. This one is not for deep
and powerful thrusting, but slow and intimate rocking.

20. Hallway Heaven

For this position, you'll need to find an area of your apartment or home with two walls that are close together, no more than a few feet apart. Have him lean his back against one wall and sink down, almost as though he's sitting. He can brace himself by putting his feet against the opposite wall or on the floor. Then you sit on top of him, facing him, and brace yourself on the wall his back is on with either your feet or your toes — depends how much strength he has to hold you there! Then you can thrust as much as you like. This one may be a bit tricky, as some strength is needed, but it allows for the excitement of spicing it up in not just a new room of your home — the living room or bedroom or kitchen counter — but an area you may never have considered a place for some sexy canoodling before.

21. Table Top

A variation on Hip Raise (position no. 18), this one gets hot quick. He'll enter you as though it's missionary position, but then you can raise your hips up to meet his pelvis. You can both control the rhythm here, for a satisfying and sensual sack session. Your partner can help to hold you up by grabbing your back as he leans forward over you. Wrap your legs around his back for deeper penetration.

22. Speed Bump

While not the most cuddly of positions, this one means things can get hot and heavy fast. Lie on your stomach and put a pillow underneath. Have your partner lie on top of you and enter you from behind. You can spread your legs for easier entry, and though he'll have to do all the work, you'll be touching what feels like everywhere.

23. The CAT

This enticing position stands for Coital Alignment Technique, and before you dismiss it as a take on the missionary — get ready for some intensely pleasurable sensations. You lie on bottom with your legs spread, and the man enters you. He pushes his body up toward your face as much as he can, so that instead of being chest-to-chest, his chest is more over your shoulders. If you tilt your hips back a bit, he can move around in small circles with constant clitoral stimulation. So instead of pushing in and out, he'll be grinding on your clitoris. The base of his penis will stimulate you while he is inside, and this should lead to an amazing orgasm, even for those who don't get them as regularly from penetrative sex.

24. Jackhammer

This one is almost like doggy style, but with some variations that will allow for a bit of adventure. You lie on your stomach, with your legs straight out behind you. He sits behind your butt, with his legs on either side of your torso. He'll need his arms behind him to get the angle right and support himself. Your partner enters you from behind, and the angle can be tricky to manage, as he'll need to tip his hips forward to connect his penis with your vagina, and you, tip your hips back. Once you get it, though, this position is an eye-opening experience.

25. Snake/Sidewinder

It's a pretty straightforward position for you and your partner to lie on your sides — but try this subtle twist on that common position. Raise whichever leg is your top leg, and help to guide his penis inside you. This position is often very intimate, with the perfect opportunity for a lot of body contact, caressing and steamy kisses. Guide your thrusting as you slowly build to climax. This position has the added bonus of a slow build, which can be much more intense once you arrive at your destination — an extra steamy, all-out orgasm that happens after much anticipation. For added control, try this one next to a wall so you can brace your feet or toes against it, and more accurately control your thrusting.

5 Bonus Oral Sex Positions

The Tilt

For him: Have your partner sit against the wall, so his back is leaning against it. He should move his feet apart so you can slide in-between them and go down on him. Between the two of you, he can move up to a more standing position, or down to more of a squatting position, and you can vary your height on your knees as well, to try out a bunch of new positions and angles.

Doggy Delight

Yep, doggy style here: Get on all fours and have your partner come at you from behind. He can lick you from behind, under, around, and you have the freedom to move your hips against his mouth to control a the sensation and speed.

Sky 69

This one is intense, but worth it! Don't worry; you'll ease into this standing 69 position slowly, but don't attempt it if he can't lift the weight of your body. The first step is for him to lie on the bed with his knees bent and legs draped over the side, feet on the floor. Get into the regular 69 position, with your mouth on his penis and your clit over his face. He'll use his abs to slowly sit up, and your legs will wrap around his head for support. He can then wrap his arms around your back, and slowly stand, when he has you secure. One crucial step here — he should turn around, facing the mattress, so if you fall, you have an easy landing pad! You may not be able to maintain this, but it sure is a fun one to try.

Spinning Top

For this sensual position, start by having your partner lie down, and you climb on top of his knees, or near his legs as you stimulate him with your mouth. After a bit of time, move your body to one side of his legs, without stopping your blow job. Then — move again, this time toward his head, so it resembles the 69 position. Then rotate one more time, to the side you haven't been on of his body. The different angles will give him different sensations in each position. Stay at one that he's really enjoying — or make it all the way around.

Facetime

As he lies on his back, you kneel above him, so that your clit is over his face. You can rock and roll in this one, helping to guide his rhythm with that of your hips. Your body is readily available for some caressing and touching as well, so don't let him be shy with grabbing your butt, breasts and letting you know how much he enjoys your body.

Thanks for Reading! (+ Bonus)

Thanks for taking the time to read our sex positions guide.

We have a great bonus offer of our companion Sex Positions Coloring Book, which is only $5.99 for a limited time.

Relax your mind and excite your body with this sensual coloring book! These 30 sex position illustrations are classy but erotic, tasteful but dirty. Let colors swirl across the pages as your imagination runs wild!

Sex Positions Coloring Book: 30 Kama Sutra Position Mandalas for Your Coloring Pleasure: only $5.99 on Amazon

BUY now at <u>bitly.com/sexycoloring</u>

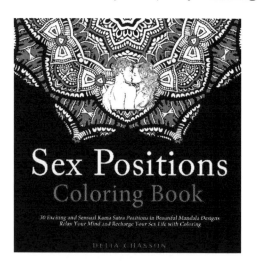

Start kinky coloring today!

Printed in Great Britain
by Amazon